THE FAT BURNING KETOGENIC DIET FOR BEGINNERS: MASTER YOUR BODY IN 10 DAYS OR LESS

Katherine Kavanagh

Text Copyright © Author

All rights reserved. No part of this cookbook may be reproduced in any form without permission in writing from the publisher except in the case of brief quotations embodied in critical articles or reviews.

Legal & Disclaimer

The information contained in this book is not designed to replace or take the place of any form of medicine or professional medical advice. The information in this book has been provided for educational and entertainment purposes only.

The information contained in this book has been compiled from sources deemed reliable, and it is accurate to the best of the Author's knowledge; however, the Author cannot guarantee its accuracy and validity and cannot be held liable for any errors or omissions. Changes are periodically made to this book. You must consult your doctor or get professional medical advice before using any of the suggested remedies, techniques, or information in this book.

Upon using the information contained in this book, you agree to hold harmless the Author from and against any damages, costs, and expenses, including any legal fees potentially resulting from the application of any of the information provided by this guide. This disclaimer applies to any damages or injury caused by the use and application, whether directly or indirectly, of any advice or information presented, whether for breach of contract, tort, negligence, personal injury, criminal intent, or under any other cause of action.

You agree to accept all risks of using the information presented inside this book. You need to consult a professional medical practitioner in order to ensure you are both able and healthy enough to participate in this program.

The Fat Burning Ketogenic Diet for Beginners

TABLE OF CONTENTS

CHAPTER 01: UNDERSTANDING KETOGENIC DIET
05

CHAPTER 02: GETTING STARTED
16

CHAPTER 03: MAKING THE KETO TRANSITION
26

CHAPTER 04: PRECIOUS KETO RECIPES FOR BEGINNERS
32

GET STARTED WITH YOUR 10-DAY KETOGENIC PLAN TODAY!
110

CONCLUSION
113

CHAPTER 01: UNDERSTANDING KETOGENIC DIET

The word "ketogenic" is derived from the word "ketosis". Ketosis refers to a natural metabolic state where the body burns its stored fat for energy instead of carbs. Much of the body's energy production comes from burning food – normally, the most preferred type of food for energy production is carbohydrates; however, when there is a limited amount of carbs in the body, it will turn to stored fats and protein for energy production.

This explains why ketogenic diets are associated with very low carbs and high fat diets. The eating plan will typically consist of foods like eggs, fish, oils, meat and green veggies. The amount of grains, cereals, pasta and bread are kept at a minimum.

In recent years, keto diets have gained a massive following among health, wellness and fitness enthusiasts because of the way it alters body functions to achieve different health goals such as weight loss. Burning of stored fat in particular is one of its strongest selling points.

HOW KETO WORKS

When you consume the standard high-carb diet, the body primarily breaks it down into molecules of fructose, glucose and galactose to provide energy for body functions. When carbs are limited in supply, the body is unable to break it down for energy and thus goes into a state of ketosis. This is a natural survival process initiated by the body when food intake is low. It triggers the production of ketones – which are energy molecules derived from the breakdown of fats in the liver. Essentially, this is the whole point and end goal of any keto diet.

Some people misconstrue this as encouraging starvation of calories. Yes, it encourages starvation; starvation of carbs; not calories. An example of a typical one day Keto meal would be as follows:

- **Breakfast:** Bacon, avocado and steamed spinach
- **Lunch:** Boiled eggs and salad with olive oil and vinegar dressing
- **Snack:** Kale chips and cheese strings
- **Dinner:** Baked salmon with mixed vegetables

You get the idea, right? So now, let's see why you need to give Keto diets a serious thought.

THE BENEFITS OF A KETO LIFESTYLE

If keto lifestyles are popular enough to draw your attention, perhaps the following reasons may convince you to give it shot.

KETO IS GREAT FOR WEIGHT LOSS

By deriving energy from stored fats, ketosis speeds up the burning of excess fat which consequently leads to weight loss. Keto may just be the answer to losing that unattractive accumulated belly fat. This is a fact supported by dozens of keto studies done on obese and overweight people in recent years.

According to Jersey Shore actor, Vinny Guadagnino, keto helped him transform his body. He says, *"When I ate sugars and grains I was 50lbs heavier and looked 10 years older. I've discovered the fountain of youth, Stop eating sugars and grains and instead 98% of the time and eat real food like whole eggs, bacon, butter, fatty steaks, fatty fish and plants"*.

KETO BOOSTS BRAIN FUNCTION

It allows the brain cells to become more efficient whilst reducing inflammation in the brain. Keto diets afford the brain the opportunity to balance the neurotransmitters called gamma-aminobutyric acid and glutamate which in turn help reduce brain fog. Clinical studies have also linked Keto to improved performance in patients with Parkinson's and Alzheimer's diseases.

KETO PROMOTES CARDIOVASCULAR HEALTH

Some people may be concerned that a Keto lifestyle promotes consumption of fats and that can't be good for the hearts. Well, here's the thing; a proper Keto diet promotes the consumption of good healthy fats such as the good cholesterol, HDL. HDL boosts all functions of the heart and improves blood circulation.

KETO INCREASES OVERALL ENDURANCE AND PERFORMANCE

We did mention before that the body likes to burn carbs as its primary source of energy. This is because it is just easier for it to do so and thus burn very quickly. However, fats and proteins burn at a much slower rate. So while carbs can give you a spike in energy, it usually lasts for a relatively short time. Energy from fats and protein lasts longer which can give you an edge to push yourself harder and longer during workouts.

KETO MAKES YOUR SKIN GLOW

The leading cause of the skin condition, acne, has been found to be poor diet riddled with a lot of sugar. Besides that, varying fluctuations in blood sugar levels has also been linked to poor skin. With keto diets, carb intake is significantly cut down hence stabilizing blood sugar in the process and dramatically improving the skin texture and outlook. Acclaimed Hollywood A-lister, Halle Berry, says (about the Keto lifestyle) that *"it is largely responsible for slowing down my ageing process"*.

Other celebrities who swear by Keto include:

- Vanessa Hudgens who says, *"I think that we've been brainwashed to think that fat is bad, but really, it's what going to make you feel fuller longer"*. Keto diet helped her lose an extra 20 pounds she had gained for a role in the movie, Gimme Shelter.

- Halle Berry, who has been type 2 diabetic since she was a teenager, says *"For years, I have been following the keto or ketogenic diet"*. This has apparently helped her manage diabetes by keeping blood glucose levels low.

- Famed Victoria Secret model, Adriana Lima maintains that she is on a *"definitely zero carbs diet"*.

- Pro-basketball player Lebron James went on a keto diet to slim down his towering 6-foot-8-inch frame back in 2014. He said in an interview that he *"didn't eat dairy, sugar, or carbohydrates for 67 days to test his mental fortitude"*.

Katherine Kavanagh

STAYING FIT ON A KETO DIET

Understanding how a keto diet works is one thing, but how do you make sure that it is a success for you? Many have tried countless times, and some have failed while others have succeeded. So what can you learn from them? What tips do you need to take with you every step of the way to make sure that you're on the right path to achieving your weight loss goal?

- **Keep track of your macros**

    Macros are the macronutrients that we get from food in the three forms that are fat, carbs and proteins. The keto diet reduces carb intake, but it is important to make sure you are getting your daily calorie requirement from the proteins and fat as well. This is why it is important to keep track of all the calories you are getting from each meal, making sure that you are not eating too little or too much.

- **Stay hydrated**

    Keep your water intake high when you are on a keto diet. When carbs are broken down, glucose is produced for energy. When fat is burned, ketones are produced. Compared to glucose, ketones are acidic. When the body has enough ketones for energy, excesses are usually flushed out throughout the kidneys. This could be stressful for the kidneys in the absence of enough water to dilute and lubricate the entire process. So keep drinking water as often as you can to reduce the stress on your kidneys.

- **Avoid or manage stress**

When on a keto diet, you want to reduce the amount of glucose (from carbs) in the blood stream, so that the body can continue relying on ketones from fat for energy. In cases where you're under stress, the hormone cortisol is produced, which triggers the increase of glucose in the blood. This in turn hinders your progress, as the body once again goes back to its preferred source of energy in glucose. Avoid this by keeping your life stress free.

- **Get in some exercise**

    Nothing complements a proven diet plan more than a good bit of exercise. In order to shape your body into the beautiful figure that you've always wanted, you're going to have to put in a bit of exercise as well. It will be covered in a later chapter, but studies have found exercise to improve the effects of a keto diet as well.

- **Plan all your meals in advance**

    When all of your meals are panned, never again will you worry about what to eat at any one point. Indecision about what to eat often times leads to unhealthy food choices, especially in people living busy lives. Having a plan helps you avoid these pitfalls because you can always monitor what you eat, and maintain a keto diet properly.

- **Keep your food keto-friendly**

    To begin your path to success with a keto diet, you are going to have to change the kind of food you have in your kitchen.

Your refrigerator and pantry should be stocked only with foods that are keto friendly. This is why the next thing we must discuss is your shopping when on a keto diet.

BUSTING COMMON MYTHS ABOUT KETO DIETS

There is a flood of information about Keto today. Some of it does not have a scientific backing to the claims. We are going to debunk some popular myths going around.

Myth #1: Your Body Does Not Need Any Carbs At All

Any keto diet that calls for 100% abandonment of carbs is misleading and should be avoided at all costs. A good keto diet advocates for low carbs and low starch. In fact, a proper keto lifestyle includes starchy vegetables in meal plans. It is not practical to deny your body and brain some carbs because they require these for optimal functioning.

Myth #2: Keto Diets Allow All Types of Fat

Just because Keto diets promote fat consumption doesn't give you the green light to consume all types of fat. Saturated fats should be avoided because of the health concerns that have been linked to them. According to the Journal of American College of Nutrition, *"replacing saturated fats with unsaturated fats such as those found in fish, nuts and seeds, will help reduce the risk of developing cardiovascular diseases and cancer"*.

Myth #3: Keto Is Bad For Athletes, Bodybuilders and Active People

This is a myth that has been propagated by proponents of high carb diets. It is true that carbs are easily burned by the body for energy but the energy source runs out quite fast. For athletes, bodybuilders and other fitness buffs, having a good source of energy that doesn't run out fast could mean the difference between posting exemplary performance and mediocre results. A lot of athletes have been found to do far better on a well-formulated keto plan.

Hopefully, the points above have helped you separate fact from fiction when dealing with the keto lifestyle.

CHAPTER 02: GETTING STARTED

Making the choice to adopt a keto lifestyle is perhaps one of the greatest decisions anyone can ever make. Those who have tried it, stand by the benefits and the results brought by the lifestyle. For a beginner who has never tried keto, it can be overwhelming to separate wheat from chaff and know what's what. This chapter aims to help you ease into the keto way of life and provide you with the relevant information you need to take off successfully.

Whether you are a beginner or seasoned veteran of the keto lifestyle you need to understand what is referred to as the 'Ketogenic Diet Hierarchy of Needs'. This is a 6-step pyramid that breaks the keto lifestyle down to help you understand, become successful and maintain success in keto. It has been summarized below.

- ❖ **Step #1: Motivation Stage**

This is the stage that addresses the "why". Having a clear understanding of what is driving you to the keto lifestyle is what is going to keep you focused. You will have to figure out what your goal is and why that goal is important to you. For example, your goal can be: *"to lose 20 pounds in 4 months"* and the purpose for the goal can be: *"so you can have more energy to spend with your loved ones"*.

- ❖ **Step #2: Knowledge Stage**

This stage involves having an understanding of what your options are, in terms of meals, when you have to eat. You can't always be preparing meals at home; so, you may want to go out dining. You should be able to tell what foods to avoid and what to prioritize.

- ❖ **Step #3: Preparation Stage**

Closely related to the previous stage, the preparation stage involves crafting out meals plans for when you are cooking at home and when you are dining out. It also deals with portioning of your meals (food groups) to the right sizes to reach ketosis.

- ❖ **Step #4: Execution Stage**

This is the stage where you begin leading a keto lifestyle. For beginners, it is likely to be a pain at first but you will soon adapt and even discover new, healthier and better-tasting foods and snacks acceptable to keto.

- ❖ **Step #5: Testing Stage**

If you are very serious about keto, then you are going to have to be testing your ketone levels periodically. Testing yourself allows you to know whether you are in ketosis or not; and if you aren't yet there, you can make the necessary adjustments, moving forward.

❖ Step #6: Mistakes and Corrections Stage

Those who have been successful with the keto lifestyle all share one thing in common; they reviewed their mistakes along the way and made corrections and refinements. While changing some habits may be almost impossible, the benefits to be reaped will remain.

ADOPTING A WINNING MINDSET FOR A KETO DIET

Any significantly life changing undertaking's success is reliant upon the mindset of the individual partaking of it. The biggest change that you will see may not even come from your body, but from how you think. If you have grown up gobbling down carbs, it is going to be a mental battle changing these ways, and you need to be prepared for it. These are the pillars of a winning mindset.

- **You have to want it**
  Don't go into keto out of peer pressure. The decision must come from you, because you want to enjoy the benefits. Picture yourself enjoying all of its amazing benefits, and internalize this image to help improve you mental fortitude.

- **Foster Discipline, Commitment and Planning**
  Commitment and discipline don't come easy. You have to keep pushing yourself every day. Remind yourself, as often as possible, of the end goal of this resolution. If you do this long enough, it will become a habit that comes naturally to you. If you have a close friend or loved one consider recruiting them. As the saying goes, *"there is strength in numbers"*.

- **Nurture Positivity**

    Nothing fuels the right mindset quite like the power of positivity. Always think positively and avoid negative thoughts that can derail you. Surround yourself with positive-thinking people. This will help you worry less, maintain focus and achieve your goals faster.

Preparing mentally will determine whether you stay in the keto way of life or give up.

STAYING FOCUSED

Now that it's clear what you need to do, all that is left is your mindset. Everything starts with the mind and a strong mind is instrumental to focus and motivation.

- **Visualize your goal**

    As former American president Theodore Roosevelt once said, "Believe you can and you're halfway there". This means that you can only achieve success if you believe in yourself.

    You have decided to try out the keto lifestyle because you want to lose weight, eat better and become healthier. Whatever your reason ultimately is, do you see yourself finally achieving it? How will you look once you've really gotten into living a better life on a keto diet?

    Visualize your goal and make it believable. A dream stops becoming impossible and becomes achievable when you break it down into manageable goals, so map out your goals and set you mind to them.

☐ Take pictures

The best way to monitor weight loss progress is by taking pictures. You do not have to measure yourself on a scale every day to see your weight because a lit of factors affect it every single day. Instead take a picture every week and see for yourself how different you look as the days go by.

Pictures are not only a great way to track progress, but a great motivator! 4 weeks in noticing your body looking a little less fat has to be one of the best feelings ever for anyone trying to shed a few pounds. It encourages you to keep working hard.

☐ Stay positive

Life is full of its ups and downs, but in the end it's how we handle these us and downs that affects our levels of positivity. Try to avoid stressful situations that could set you back by increasing cortisol levels, and find ways to make yourself more relaxed, happy and stress free. It's not only good for the body, but also important to your overall mentality as you get into the keto lifestyle.

- **Find support**

Former Journalist Mark Shieds once said, "There is always strength in numbers". The more there are people around you practicing the same diet as you, the more motivating it is to you. It is a source of emotional support that can keep you going even in times when it gets challenging. Find communities of people on their own weight loss journeys with the keto diet and together the moral support will always motivate you.

NOTE

Your First 7 Days Are Important!

When you begin getting adjusted to your new keto diet, the first week is probably going to be the most important. This is because your body will be undergoing drastic changes as it switches from one preferred fuel source to another. Some important things to do during this time include

- ☐ Make a shopping list of all the food you're going to need to restock your kitchen at the start of the week, possibly even before. Pick a day to go shopping as well, preferably as soon as is possible.

- ☐ Reduce or go easy on your exercises this week. Your body will be changing and your routine may suffer for it. Take it easy and don't strain yourself.

- ☐ Note down everything you have eaten every day, and how many calories you've consumed. You can use a notebook or get a tracking app for your phone. Always remember to note everything to help keep close track of your keto journey.

- Remember to drink a lot of water every day as your body goes into ketosis and even long afterwards. This helps to relieve ketosis symptoms significantly.

Remember that if you make it past these first 7 days successfully, then you are already on your way to enjoying the full keto lifestyle, so keep on keeping on!

# CHAPTER 03: MAKING THE KETO TRANSITION

PANTRY MAKEOVER

You already know that keto promotes low-carb and high-fat diets. This section outlines foods to eat, avoid and replace when practicing the ketogenic diet; so, let's get to it.

FOODS TO EAT

Dairy Products

- Yogurt
- Butter
- Cream
- Cheeses
- Milk

Meats and Other Proteins

- Poultry
- Beef and other red meats
- Pork
- Fish (Both Sea and Inland Fish)

- Eggs

Low Starch Vegetables and Low-Sugar Fruits

- Broccoli
- Kale
- Tomatoes
- Mushrooms
- Avocado
- Eggplants
- Bell Peppers
- Cauliflower
- Berries
- Lemon and limes

Nuts and Seeds

- Most nuts are acceptable

FOODS TO AVOID

Grains, Cereals, Legumes, Pastas and Breads

- Wheat
- Barley
- Rice
- Oats
- Quinoa
- Rye
- Corn
- Millet
- Sorghum
- Bulgur

- Amaranth
- Buckwheat
- Beans
- Sprouted Grains

High-Sugar Fruits and Juices

- Bananas
- Pineapples
- Grapes
- Apples
- Mangoes
- Tangerines
- Papaya
- Fruit smoothies

Starchy Vegetables

- Potatoes
- Butternut Squash
- Sweet potatoes
- Peas
- Pumpkin
- Yams
- Yucca
- Parsnips

FOODS TO REPLACE

The table below contains a list of swaps you can make for your recipes and meals

Food	Keto Substitute
Flour	Almond flour
Bread	Pork rinds
Tortillas	Lettuce leaves
Rice	Cauliflower rice
Sugar	Stevia
Coffee	Bulletproof coffee
Mashed potatoes	Mashed cauliflower
Burger buns	Portobello mushrooms
Spaghetti	Spaghetti squash
Pasta	Veggie noodles
Potato chips	Kale chips
Pancakes	Cream cheese pancakes

Going Shopping

We've already established that the food in your home needs to be keto friendly in order for you to successfully this diet. You're going to have to go shopping for this new kitchen makeover, and the following tips should make your life that much easier.

- **Get a scale**

    Since you are going to be planning a lot of your meals and keeping track of your macros, you're going to be weighing your food a lot of the time. This is why the scale may be the single most important part of your kitchen on a keto diet. Invest in a good scale to make your tracking much easier.

- **Never shop when you're hungry**

    Always make sure that you're on a full stomach whenever you're going shopping. Hunger can be your worst enemy in a grocery store or supermarket, because it will tempt your impulse buying instincts into purchasing unhealthy food to sate your hunger a soon as possible. This could set your healthy keto eating diet habits back before they even properly take off.

- **Buy things in bulk where possible**

    Not only does bulk buying save you on costs, it also allows you to better plan your meals by having them in stock whenever you need them for meal ideas that are days away.

- **Focus on healthy food items when you shop**

    Healthy food choices are keto-friendly choices. As you shop focus on healthy fats which will be described in better detail in the next chapter. Prioritize healthy proteins such as grass-fed beef. Get your micronutrients from eating a lot of vegetables as well. If you must sweeten your food, then select sweeteners that do not raise your blood glucose.

CHAPTER 04: PRECIOUS KETO RECIPES FOR BEGINNERS

DAY 1

Breakfast: Avocado Bacon Deviled Eggs

Yield: 12 egg halves (2 servings as a meal or 3 servings as a snack)

This is one of the best portable snacks to bring with you to a party or other event. Everyone loves deviled eggs, keto or not! I have provided macronutrient information for eating them as a meal or as a fat bomb snack.

Nutritional info

As a meal

Calories 610, fat 53, fiber 2, carbs 4, protein 28

As a snack

Calories 399, fat 34, fiber 1.6, carbs 2.6, protein 19

Ingredients:

- 6 slices bacon
- 6 eggs

Katherine Kavanagh

- [ ] ½ medium-sized ripe avocado
- [ ] 5 tablespoons (2.5 ounces/70 g) mayonnaise
- [ ] ½ teaspoon fine sea salt
- [ ] Ground black pepper
- [ ] Paprika, for garnish (optional)

Directions:

i. In a skillet over medium heat, fry the bacon until slightly crispy, 3 to 5 minutes. Set aside.

ii. In a small pan of water over high heat, boil the eggs for 6 minutes. Remove from the heat and immerse in cold water until cool. Drain and peel. Cut each egg in half lengthwise. Place the yolks in a bowl.

iii. Add the avocado to the bowl with the egg yolks. Add the mayonnaise, salt, and pepper to taste. Mash together with a fork or an immersion blender until smooth and creamy.

iv. Finely chop the bacon. Add about half to the bowl of filling and mix together.

v. Fill a piping bag with the egg yolk mixture. Pipe the filling evenly into the egg white halves. Garnish with the remaining chopped

---

Tip

Don't have a piping bag? Fill a re-sealable plastic bag with the filling. Move the filling to one lower corner of the bag and snip off that corner, about ¼ inches (6 mm) from the end. Use the plastic bag as you would a piping bad to squeeze the filling into each egg white half.

bacon and paprika, if desired. Serve at room temperature or chilled.

Lunch: Coconut Soup

Yield: 4 servings

This creamy soup is the quintessential Thai soup. Thai cuisine makes the most of fragrant spices and incorporates saturated fat–filled coconut milk in wonderful ways, and this soup is no exception. It features the full spectrum of what makes Thai food so tasty—sweet, sour, salty, and spicy flavors.

Nutritional info

Calories 486, fat 42, fiber 2, carbs 10, protein 20

Ingredients:

- 5 cups (40 fluid ounces/1.2 L) chicken bone broth
- 2 (1- to 2-inch/2.5- to 5-cm) pieces galangal, sliced
- 2 shallots, sliced
- 2 stalks lemon grass

- [ ] 8 kaffir lime leaves
- [ ] 6 ounces (170 g) boneless, skinless chicken breast, thinly sliced
- [ ] 8 ounces (225 g) white mushrooms, sliced
- [ ] 4 cups (32 ounces/1 L) coconut cream
- [ ] 10 cherry tomatoes, halved
- [ ] 1 red chili pepper, sliced in half lengthwise (optional)
- [ ] 1 tablespoon freshly squeezed lime juice
- [ ] 1 tablespoon fish sauce
- [ ] 2 to 4 drops liquid stevia, to taste
- [ ] ¼ cup (1 ounce/30 g) fresh cilantro leaves

Directions:

i. Bring the broth and galangal to a boil in a medium saucepan over high heat. Reduce the heat to a simmer and cook until the broth absorbs the flavor of the galangal, 25 to 30 minutes.

ii. Add the shallots, lemon grass, and lime leaves. Reduce the heat to medium-low and add the chicken and mushrooms; simmer for 15 to 20 minutes, until the chicken is cooked.

iii. Add the coconut cream, tomatoes, chili pepper (if using), lime juice, fish sauce, and stevia. Cook for 4 to 5 minutes more, until

---

Tip

You can make this soup with shrimp instead of chicken which is equally delicious. To make it a full meal, add some shirataki noodles.

the flavors are well combined. Remove from the heat and top with the cilantro.

Dinner: Steak with Béarnaise Sauce

Yield: 4 servings

My recipe for béarnaise sauce makes about 1 1/4 cups, so you'll have a little extra. No worries! Béarnaise turns any meat dish into a heavenly preparation, so it's nice to have extra on hand. Store leftover sauce in the fridge for up to 6 days and revive it with 1 tablespoon of ice-cold water.

Nutritional info

Calories 723, fat 64.5, fiber 4, carbs 4, protein 36

Ingredients:

- 4 (6-ounce/170-g) boneless rib-eye steaks
- Sea salt and ground black pepper
- 24 asparagus spears, woody ends trimmed
- 3/4 cup plus 2 tablespoons (7 fluid ounces/210 ml) Béarnaise Sauce

Directions:

i. Preheat a grill to medium-high heat.

ii. Prepare the steaks for grilling by seasoning them on both sides with salt and pepper. Grill the steaks for 4 to 5 minutes on each side for medium-done steaks, or to your desired level of doneness. Let rest for about 10 minutes.

iii. In a wide, deep pan over high heat, bring 4 to 5 cups of water to a boil. Add the asparagus and turn off the heat, leaving the pan on the burner. Leave the asparagus in the hot water for 3 to 4 minutes, until bright green. Remove from the water and set aside to drain.

iv. Serve each steak with 6 stalks of asparagus and 3½ tablespoons of the béarnaise sauce.

Dessert: Lemon Curd

Yield: 4 servings

With only seven ingredients, it is such an easy dessert to make, but the shot glasses are a wow factor for entertaining. Try different sweeteners if you prefer. Most of the carbs in this recipe come from the erythritol, which I count; however, many people do not count the carbs in erythritol, as it is a fiber-based sweetener. I understand this logic; however, because erythritol is made from sugar in a chemical process, in my opinion it's important to count those carbs.

Nutritional info

Calories 148, fat 15, fiber 3.3, carbs 2.9, protein 2.3

Ingredients:

- 3 egg yolks
- 3/8 cup (3 fluid ounces/87.5 ml) freshly squeezed lemon juice
- ¼ cup (2 ounces/57.5 g) erythritol, ground in a small food processor until powdery
- ½ to 1 teaspoon liquid stevia, to taste
- Pinch of fine sea salt
- ¼ cup (2 ounces/57.5g) unsalted butter, cut into 1/2-inch (1.25-cm) cubes
- 1 teaspoon grated lemon zest

Directions:

i. In a small heavy saucepan, whisk together the egg yolks, lemon juice, erythritol, stevia, and salt. Cook over medium heat, whisking constantly, until it coats the back of a wooden spoon, 6 to 7 minutes.

ii. Remove the pan from the heat and add the butter, stirring as it melts.

iii. Pour the curd into eight 2-ounce (30-ml) shot glasses, 8 small ramekins, or a serving bowl and place in the refrigerator to chill completely, 1 to 2 hours or overnight. Store in the refrigerator for up to 5 days.

> **Tip**
>
> For an even prettier presentation, top the lemon curd with some shredded coconut and fresh berries.

DAY 2

Breakfast: BULLETPROOF COFFEE / TEA

Lunch: Three-Cheese Macaroni

Yield: 4 servings

The Fat Burning Ketogenic Diet for Beginners

This recipe uses a French sauce called béchamel as a base, but substitutes keto-friendly almond flour for the traditional all-purpose flour. Just like the quick and easy boxed version, this dish is made entirely on the stovetop, although there is a short broiling step to get the top brown and delicious. If you can't find macaroni-style shirataki noodles, use the fettuccine style and cut them into 1-inch (2.5-cm) pieces.

Nutritional info

Calories 622, fat 58.5, fiber 3, carbs 4.8, protein 21

Ingredients:

- [ ] 4 (7-ounce/200-g) packages macaroni-style zero-carb shirataki noodles
- [ ] 6 slices bacon
- [ ] ¾ cup (6 ounces/170 g) unsalted butter
- [ ] ¼ cup plus 2 tablespoons (1½ ounces/40 g) almond flour
- [ ] 1 cup (8 fluid ounces/240 ml) almond milk, warmed
- [ ] 1 cup (8 ounces/230 g) shredded Gruyère cheese
- [ ] ½ cup (4 ounces/115 g) shredded cheddar cheese
- [ ] 1 teaspoon onion powder
- [ ] ½ teaspoon coarse sea salt
- [ ] ¼ teaspoon ground nutmeg

- ¼ cup (1 ounce/28 g) grated Parmesan cheese

Directions:

i. Rinse and drain the noodles. In a saucepan over high heat, boil the noodles in water for 1 to 2 minutes. Drain and set on paper towels to absorb the excess water.

ii. In a medium skillet over medium heat, fry the bacon for 4 to 5 minutes, until medium crisp; remove to a cutting board to cool. Slice or crumble the bacon into rough bits and set aside.

iii. In a medium saucepan over medium-low heat, melt the butter. Add the almond flour and stir to combine. Continue to cook, stirring frequently, for 1 to 2 minutes, until well combined and smooth and starting to bubble lightly.

iv. Slowly pour in the almond milk, combining well with a whisk.

v. Add the Gruyère and cheddar and stir until just melted, then remove from the heat. Stir in the onion powder, salt, and nutmeg.

vi. In a bowl, combine the noodles and sauce. Divide the sauced noodles between 4 individual oven-safe ramekins or 1 large baking dish. Top evenly with the Parmesan.

vii. Set the oven to broil and broil the macaroni for 3 to 4 minutes, until a browned crust forms. Top with the crumbled bacon before serving.

Tip

You can find zero-carb shirataki noodles at health-food stores or online.

Dinner: Feta-Stuffed Meatballs

Yield: 4 servings

I love meatloaf with warm, melty goat cheese in the center, so I decided to create a version with meatballs for a fun way to enjoy the same flavor profile in a different form. With feta, Kalamata olives, and tomato sauce, this recipe features a Mediterranean/Greek twist.

Nutritional info

Calories 621, fat 50.5, fiber 3, carbs 8.3, protein 36.3

Ingredients:

FETA-STUFFED MEATBALLS:

- ½ cup (2 ounces/55 g) almond flour
- ¼ cup (1 ounce/27 g) grated red onions
- ¼ cup (11/4 ounces/35 g) finely chopped Kalamata olives
- 2 tablespoons finely chopped fresh parsley
- 1 egg, lightly whisked
- 3 cloves garlic, minced

- ☐ ½ teaspoon fine sea salt
- ☐ ¼ teaspoon ground black pepper
- ☐ ¼ teaspoon ground nutmeg
- ☐ 1 pound (455 g) ground beef
- ☐ 6 ounces (170 g) firm feta cheese

GREEK TOMATO SAUCE:

- ☐ 2 cups (11 ounces/315 g) chopped plum tomatoes
- ☐ 1/3 cup (23/4 fluid ounces/80 ml) olive oil
- ☐ 1 teaspoon dried oregano leaves
- ☐ 1 teaspoon fine sea salt
- ☐ ¼ teaspoon red pepper flakes
- ☐ ¼ teaspoon ground black pepper

Directions:

i. Preheat the oven to 400°F (205°C).

ii. Make the meatballs: In a bowl, stir together the flour, onions, olives, parsley, egg, garlic, salt, pepper, and nutmeg. Crumble in the ground beef and mix with your hands until just combined. Divide into 20 equal portions and roll into 2-inch (5-cm) balls.

iii. Cut the feta into twenty ½-inch (1.25-cm) cubes. Gently press a feta cube into the center of each meatball and close the meat around the cheese. Place the feta-filled meatballs in a 13 by 9-inch (33 by 23-cm) glass baking dish.

iv. Make the tomato sauce: In a food processor or blender, pulse all the sauce ingredients until pureed. Pour the sauce over the meatballs.

v. Bake, uncovered, until the meatballs reach an internal temperature of 160°F (71°C), 25 to 30 minutes. The oils will rise to the top of the sauce. If desired, remove the meatballs from the dish and re-emulsify the sauce with an immersion blender. Serve the sauce over the meatballs.

Dessert: Cinnamon Custard

Yield: 2 servings

Nutritional info

Using erythritol and liquid stevia

Calories 251, fat 50.5, fiber 6.5, carbs 9.5, protein 6.5

Using liquid stevia only

Calories 259, fat 24, fiber 1, carbs 4, protein 6.5

Ingredients:

- ☐ 1 cup (8 ounces/225 g) coconut cream
- ☐ 1 cup (8 fluid ounces/240 ml) almond milk
- ☐ 1 egg
- ☐ 1 tablespoon erythritol or powdered stevia (optional)
- ☐ 1 teaspoon vanilla extract
- ☐ ½ teaspoon liquid stevia
- ☐ ¼ teaspoon ground Ceylon cinnamon or regular cinnamon
- ☐ ¼ teaspoon ground nutmeg (optional)
- ☐ Pinch of sea salt
- ☐ 1 or 2 drops almond extract, to taste

> **Note**
> If you forget to chill the cans of coconut milk ahead of time (allowing the cream to separate from the milk), you can use the same amount of room-temperature full-fat coconut milk. The custard will have a slightly higher carb content when made with coconut milk.

Directions:

i. Preheat the oven to 325°F (163°C).
ii. In a blender, blend all the ingredients until smooth.
iii. Place two 1-cup (240-ml) ramekins in a deep ovenproof baking dish. Divide the custard between the ramekins. Pour boiling water into the baking dish until it comes about halfway up the sides of the ramekins.
iv. Bake for 1 hour, until set but still a bit jellylike in the center. Let cool slightly and then serve warm, or place in the refrigerator to chill before serving.

DAY 3

Breakfast: Baked Eggs Benedict Casserole

Yield: 3 servings

This delicious egg bake tastes just like eggs Benny but is easier to prepare, especially when serving guests. You may make it 24 hours ahead of time and then reheat it in the oven, covered with aluminum foil or a lid, for 15 to 20 minutes before serving. This casserole is traditionally made with English muffins; feel free to enhance this version with keto bread slices or zero-carb English muffins.

Nutritional info

Calories 645, fat 55.7, fiber 0.3, carbs 2, protein 31

Ingredients:

- 6 ounces (170g) bacon, chopped
- 3 eggs
- 1 cup (8 fluid ounces/237.5 ml) almond milk
- ½ tablespoon finely chopped fresh chives or dill
- ½ tablespoon chopped fresh parsley
- ¼ teaspoon onion powder
- ¼ teaspoon fine sea salt
- Pinch ground black pepper
- Pinch paprika
- ½ batch Hollandaise, for serving
- Hot sauce, for serving (optional)

Directions:

i. Preheat the oven to 375°F (190°C).

ii. Layer the bacon in the bottom of a 9-inch (23-cm) square baking dish.

iii. In a bowl, whisk together the eggs, milk, chives, parsley, onion powder, salt, pepper, and paprika.

iv. Pour the egg mixture over the bacon. Cover with an ovenproof lid or aluminum foil.

v. Bake, covered, for 25 to 30 minutes. Remove the lid and bake for another 10 to 15 minutes, until a toothpick or knife inserted in the center comes out clean.

vi. Remove the casserole from the oven and let cool slightly before cutting. Serve each portion drizzled with 3⅓ tablespoons of the hollandaise and a little hot sauce, if desired.

Lunch: Bacon Pesto Pasta

Yield: 1 serving

This is one of the easiest recipes, requiring only a handful of ingredients and only 20 minutes from start to finish. You will need only half of the pesto; save the rest for use as a dip, a topper for eggs, a condiment for burgers, or anything that needs a little pizzazz. Pesto is traditionally made with basil, pine nuts, Parmesan cheese, and olive oil, but I've updated the recipe with power-packed MCT oil and kale for antioxidants and vitamin C. If you like a creamier, even cheesier pesto, use cashews along with or instead of the pine nuts. This is a super-keto recipe, with the MCT oil generating fat burning ketones and the macronutrient percentages being on target. It is delicious and extremely satiating for all-day fuel.

Warning: You may not be able to finish it all!

Nutritional info

Calories 808, fat 77, fiber 3, carbs 9, protein 25

Ingredients:

- 1 (7-ounce/200-g) package angel hair–style or other long zero-carb shirataki noodles
- 6 slices bacon

PESTO:

- 1 cup (1 ounce/30 g) fresh basil leaves
- ½ cup (1 ounce/35 g) stemmed and chopped fresh kale
- ½ cup (2½ ounces/70 g) pine nuts or raw cashews
- ½ cup (4 fluid ounces/120 ml) MCT oil
- 1½ tablespoons grated Parmesan cheese

The Fat Burning Ketogenic Diet for Beginners

- ☐ 1 clove garlic, or ¼ teaspoon garlic powder
- ☐ ½ teaspoon fine sea salt
- ☐ Ground black pepper, to taste

FOR GARNISH:

- ☐ 1½ teaspoons grated or shaved Parmesan cheese
- ☐ Toasted pine nuts

Directions:

i. Rinse and drain the noodles. In a saucepan over high heat, boil the noodles in water for 1 to 2 minutes. Drain and set on paper towels to absorb the excess water.

ii. In a medium skillet over medium heat, fry the bacon for 3 to 4 minutes, until cooked but not crispy. Chop into ½-inch (1.25-cm) pieces.

iii. Place the pesto ingredients in a food processor and process until fully combined and smooth.

iv. Add the noodles to the skillet with the bacon and cook over medium heat for 1 to 2 minutes to remove any remaining moisture. Add half of the pesto to the pan and mix well; reserve

---

Note

If you like a strong garlic flavor, add raw garlic to the pesto. If you prefer a milder flavor, use garlic powder. You can also add sautéed kale to this

the remainder for another use. Plate the sauced noodles and garnish with Parmesan and toasted pine nuts.

Dinner: Thai Chicken Satay

Yield: 4 servings

Satay sauce is traditionally made with peanut butter and sugar. I've replaced those ingredients here with almond butter and natural sweetener for all the flavor without the sugar. This recipe is cooked on skewers, and you can use metal or bamboo. If you use bamboo skewers, you will need to soak them in water for 30 minutes prior to grilling.

Nutritional info

Calories 511, fat 42.5, fiber 2.5, carbs 5.5, protein 25

Ingredients:

- ☐ 1 pound (455 g) boneless chicken breasts, preferably skin-on, cubed
- ☐ 2 tablespoons coconut oil, melted
- ☐ 2 cups (4 ounces/115 g) shredded iceberg lettuce
- ☐ Lime wedges, for serving (optional)

SATAY SAUCE:

- ¾ cup (6 ounces/170 g) coconut cream
- ¼ cup (2 ounces/55 g) unsweetened almond butter
- 2 tablespoons crushed almonds
- 1 tablespoon apple cider vinegar
- 1 tablespoon fish sauce
- 1 tablespoon freshly squeezed lime juice
- 1 tablespoon red curry paste
- 1 tablespoon tamari
- 1 tablespoon erythritol, or ½ teaspoon liquid stevia (optional)

Directions:

i. Divide the cubed chicken between 8 skewers. Use a brush to coat the chicken well with the coconut oil.

ii. If using a grill, preheat the grill to medium heat. Grill the chicken skewers for 5 to 6 minutes, flip, and grill for another 5 to 6 minutes. Alternatively, you can use a stovetop grill pan over medium heat, cooking for 5 to 6 minutes on each side. The chicken will be white all the way through when finished.

iii. Meanwhile, in a medium saucepan over low heat, stir together all the satay sauce ingredients until well blended, 3 to 4 minutes.

iv. Place one-quarter of the lettuce on each of 4 plates. Divide the chicken skewers between the plates. Top the chicken with the satay sauce, or serve the sauce on the side as a dip. Serve with lime wedges, if desired.

Dessert: Chocolate Mint Mousse

Yield: 4 servings

Nutritional info

Calories 216, fat 20, fiber 4.5, carbs 7, protein 4

Ingredients:

- 1½ cups (12 ounces/340 g) coconut cream
- 1½ cups (12 fluid ounces/350 ml) almond milk
- 2 tablespoons unsweetened cocoa powder
- ½ teaspoon liquid stevia
- ¼ teaspoon vanilla extract
- 2 to 4 drops peppermint extract, to taste
- Pinch of sea salt

- ☐ 1 1/2 teaspoons chopped fresh mint, plus 4 small sprigs for garnish
- ☐ 3 tablespoons chia seeds

> **Note**
> If you forget to chill the cans of coconut milk ahead of time (allowing the cream to separate from the milk), you can use the same amount of room-temperature full-fat coconut milk. The mousse will have a slightly higher carb content when made with coconut milk.

Directions:

i. In a blender, blend the cream, milk, cocoa powder, stevia, extracts, salt, and chopped mint. Pour into a mixing bowl and add the chia seeds; mix well. Divide the mixture between 4 individual serving bowls, glasses, or ramekins.

ii. Chill in the refrigerator for 1 to 2 hours or overnight to allow the chia seeds to bloom and the mousse to set; overnight is ideal.

iii. When ready to serve, remove the mousse from the refrigerator and garnish with the mint sprigs.

DAY 4

Breakfast: BULLETPROOF COFFEE / TEA

Lunch: Pasta Bolognese

Yield: 4 servings

I like to serve this Bolognese on shirataki noodles. You can also serve it over shredded green cabbage or zucchini noodles.

Nutritional info

Calories 563, fat 47.8, fiber 2.3, carbs 5.3, protein 28

Ingredients:

- ☐ 5 slices bacon
- ☐ 4 (7-ounce/200-g) packages spaghetti-style zero-carb
- ☐ shirataki noodles
- ☐ 5 ounces (140 g) ground beef
- ☐ 5 ounces (140 g) ground pork
- ☐ ½ cup (4 ounces/115 g) butter
- ☐ ¼ cup chopped onions
- ☐ 1 clove garlic, minced
- ☐ 1 medium tomato, chopped

- 1 tablespoon chopped fresh parsley, plus more for garnish
- 1 tablespoon dried marjoram leaves
- 1 tablespoon dried oregano leaves
- ½ teaspoon fine sea salt
- ¼ teaspoon ground black pepper
- 2 tablespoons grated Parmesan cheese, for garnish

Directions:

i. In a medium skillet over medium heat, fry the bacon for 3 to 4 minutes, until cooked but not crispy. Remove from the pan and set aside, leaving the bacon fat in the pan.

ii. Rinse and drain the noodles. In a saucepan over high heat, boil the noodles in water for 1 to 2 minutes. Drain and set on paper towels to absorb the excess water.

iii. In the skillet you used to cook the bacon, brown the ground beef and pork, breaking apart the meat with a wooden spoon as it cooks, 7 to 8 minutes.

iv. In a saucepan over medium heat, melt the butter. Add the onions and garlic and sauté until lightly cooked, 3 to 4 minutes. Add the tomato and stir to combine.

v. Add the ground meat and bacon to the onion mixture and mix together. Add the parsley, marjoram, oregano, salt, and pepper and stir again. Simmer for 5 minutes to warm through.

vi. Serve the sauce over the noodles, sprinkled with the Parmesan and chopped parsley.

Dinner: Steak with Green Peppercorn Sauce

Yield: 2 servings

I first had this dish in Italy and fell in love. The lush steak sauce in this dish makes any night of the week a special occasion! The recipe traditionally calls for brandy, but here I use apple cider vinegar as a replacement.

Nutritional info

Calories 667, fat 57.5, fiber 1.5, carbs 4, protein 31

Ingredients:

- ¼ cup (13/4 ounces/50 g) green peppercorns in brine, well drained
- 4 tablespoons (2 ounces/55 g) butter, divided
- 2 (5-ounce/140-g) boneless sirloin steaks (3/4 inch/2 cm thick)
- 2 tablespoons minced shallots or green onions
- ½ cup (4 fluid ounces/120 ml) beef bone broth
- ¼ cup (2 fluid ounces/60 ml) apple cider vinegar

- [ ] 1 tablespoon tamari
- [ ] ½ cup (4 fluid ounces/120 ml) heavy whipping cream
- [ ] ¼ teaspoon fine sea salt
- [ ] Fresh watercress, for garnish (optional)

Directions:

i. Preheat the oven to 200°F (95°C).

ii. In a mortar and pestle or using a food processor, crush the peppercorns to a paste.

iii. In a skillet over medium-high heat, melt 2 tablespoons of the butter. Increase the heat to high and sear the steaks for 4 to 5 minutes on each side for medium-done steaks, or to your desired level of doneness. Remove from the pan and keep warm.

iv. In the same skillet over medium heat, melt the remaining 2 tablespoons of butter. Add the shallots and peppercorn paste, scraping the pan to combine them with the steak drippings.

v. Pour in the broth, vinegar, and tamari and bring to a boil. Reduce the heat and simmer until the liquid has reduced by half, 5 to 6 minutes. Add the cream and salt and stir to combine.

vi. Serve the sauce over the steaks and garnish with watercress, if desired.

Dessert: Instant Chia Pudding

Yield: 4 servings

Chia pudding is a wonderful keto staple.

Nutritional info

Calories 291, fat 27.7, fiber 4.5, carbs 6, protein 31

- **Ingredients:**
- 1½ cups (12 ounces/340 g) coconut cream
- 1½ cups (12 fluid ounces/350 ml) almond milk
- ½ teaspoon liquid stevia
- ¼ teaspoon almond extract
- ¼ teaspoon vanilla extract
- Pinch of sea salt
- ¼ cup (1 1/2 ounces/38 g) chia seeds
- Ground Ceylon cinnamon or regular cinnamon, for garnish
- Raw pumpkin seeds, for garnish (optional)

> **Note**
>
> If you forget to chill the cans of coconut milk ahead of time (allowing the cream to separate from the milk), you can use the same amount of room-temperature full-fat coconut milk. The pudding will have a slightly higher carb content when made with coconut milk.

Directions:

i. In a blender, blend all the ingredients except the chia seeds and garnishes. Pour into a mixing bowl and add the chia seeds; mix well.

ii. Divide the pudding mixture between 4 individual serving bowls, glasses, or small ramekins.

iii. Chill in the refrigerator for 1 to 2 hours or overnight to allow the chia seeds to bloom and the pudding to set; overnight is ideal.

iv. When ready to serve, remove from the refrigerator and sprinkle with cinnamon and a few pumpkin seeds, if desired.

DAY 5

Breakfast: Breakfast Crêpes

Yield: 6 crêpes (2 per serving)

I grew up on my mother's delicious English crêpes. They always seemed like such an indulgence with the flour, butter, and sugar! This version is so healthy, nutritious, and ketogenic that you could enjoy them every day.

Nutritional info

Calories 277, fat 23.3, fiber 2, carbs 3.7, protein 11.3

Ingredients:

- ☐ 5 eggs
- ☐ ⅔ cup (5⅓ fluid ounces/160 ml) almond milk
- ☐ 2 tablespoons coconut flour
- ☐ 3 or 4 drops liquid stevia
- ☐ ¼ teaspoon almond extract
- ☐ ¼ teaspoon vanilla extract
- ☐ 3 tablespoons coconut oil or unsalted butter, for the pan

FOR SERVING (OPTIONAL):

- ☐ Butter

- ☐ Ground Ceylon cinnamon or regular cinnamon
- ☐ Freshly squeezed lemon juice
- ☐ Powdered stevia

Directions:

i. Using an electric mixer, beat together the eggs, milk, coconut flour, stevia, and extracts until well incorporated.

ii. In a small skillet over high heat, melt the coconut oil.

iii. Pour ¼ cup of the batter into the pan to make a crêpe, rotating the pan to spread the batter into a thin layer. When cooked on one side (about 1 minute), flip and cook on the other side. Remove from the pan and keep warm. Repeat with the remaining batter, making a total of 6 crêpes.

iv. If desired, serve the crêpes with butter and cinnamon or with lemon juice and stevia.

Lunch: Fettuccine Alfredo with Grilled Shrimp

Yield: 4 servings

My favorite Italian dish has always been fettuccine Alfredo. Between the rich cream and the decadent noodles, I always thought of it as an excessively indulgent dish, to be ordered once a year on a special occasion—if that. With zero-carb shirataki noodles, however, you can enjoy this rich and creamy dish without guilt.

Nutritional info

Calories 574, fat 54.5, fiber 4, carbs 4.5, protein 22.8

Ingredients:

- 4 (7-ounce/200-g) packages fettuccine-style zero-carb shirataki noodles
- 2 ounces (55 g) pancetta, diced
- ½ cup (4 ounces/115 g) butter
- 1 (8-ounce/225-g) package cream cheese
- 1 cup (8 fluid ounces/240 ml) heavy whipping cream
- ½ cup plus 2 tablespoons (2½ ounces/70 g) grated Parmesan cheese, divided
- 2 cloves garlic, minced
- ½ teaspoon fine sea salt
- ¼ teaspoon ground black pepper
- 20 large uncooked frozen or fresh shrimp, thawed, peeled, and deveined

The Fat Burning Ketogenic Diet for Beginners

Directions:

i. Rinse and drain the noodles. In a saucepan over high heat, boil the noodles in water for 1 to 2 minutes. Drain and set on paper towels to absorb the excess water.

ii. Place the noodles a cutting board and chop into 1-inch (2.5-cm) segments.

iii. In a skillet over medium heat, fry the pancetta for 3 to 4 minutes, until cooked but not crisp. Slide the pan off the heat.

iv. In a saucepan over low heat, melt the butter. Add the cream cheese, heavy cream, ½ cup of the Parmesan, garlic, salt, and pepper. Cook, stirring frequently, until the sauce starts to bubble; remove from the heat and cover to keep warm.

v. Return the pan with the pancetta to the stovetop over medium-low heat. Add the shrimp to the pan and cook for 2 to 3 minutes, until the shrimp is bright pink, being careful not to overcook. Remove from the heat.

vi. Add the noodles to the Alfredo sauce and mix until the noodles are well coated. Divide between 4 plates. Top each plate with one-quarter of the pancetta and shrimp, and then sprinkle each plate with 1½ teaspoons of the remaining Parmesan.

Dinner: Duck Rillettes

Yield: 6 servings

This is an amazing "dip" or pâté-like dish! I love it with fermented pickles, sauerkraut. This treat is very keto, with 80 percent fat and only 1 percent total carb.

Nutritional info

Calories 457, fat 40, fiber 0.3, carbs 1.3, protein 23

Ingredients:

- ☐ 4 duck legs
- ☐ ½ cup (4 ounces/115 g) duck fat, melted
- ☐ 3 cloves garlic, minced
- ☐ 1 tablespoon chopped fresh thyme
- ☐ 1 bay leaf
- ☐ ½ teaspoon fine sea salt
- ☐ ¼ teaspoon ground black pepper
- ☐ 2 tablespoons apple cider vinegar
- ☐ ¾ cup (6 fluid ounces/180 ml) duck fat from cooking
- ☐ 2 tablespoons thinly sliced green onions
- ☐ ⅛ teaspoon ground cloves

- ☐ ⅛ teaspoon ground Ceylon cinnamon or regular cinnamon
- ☐ ⅛ teaspoon ground nutmeg
- ☐ 1 tablespoon grated orange zest
- ☐ ½ teaspoon ginger juice, or 1 teaspoon grated fresh ginger
- ☐ 2 to 4 drops liquid stevia, or 1 teaspoon erythritol

Directions:

i. Preheat the oven to 300°F (150°C).

ii. Place the duck legs in a roasting pan. Rub the melted duck fat, garlic, thyme, bay leaf, salt, and pepper into the skin of the duck.

iii. Add the vinegar to the pan. Cover with aluminum foil and bake for about 2 hours, until the meat is tender and falling off the bone.

iv. Let cool, then pull the meat and skin from the bones with a fork. Remove ¾ cup (6 ounces/180 ml) of duck fat from the roasting pan and place it in a mixing bowl.

v. To the bowl with the duck fat, add the shredded meat and skin, along with the remaining ingredients. Toss everything together to combine. Divide between six ½-cup (4-ounce/115-g) ramekins and refrigerate for 1 hour or until the fat has solidified.

Dessert: Cheesecake Fat Bombs

Yield: 4 servings

These are super-quick and easy fat bombs that you make using a stand mixer. With the added coconut oil, and at 91 percent fat and only 2 grams of carbs per serving, they are very ketogenic. Make sure to take the cream cheese and butter out of the fridge ahead of time.

Nutritional info

Calories 319, fat 30.8, fiber 0, carbs 2, protein 4

Ingredients:

- 1 (8-ounce/225-g) package cream cheese, softened
- 2 tablespoons butter, softened
- 2 tablespoons coconut oil, softened
- 1 teaspoon liquid stevia
- 1 teaspoon vanilla extract, or 1 tablespoon freshly squeezed lemon juice
- Pinch of sea salt
- Unsweetened coconut flakes, toasted, for garnish (optional)

> **Note**
>
> For a different flavor, try blueberry, raspberry, or any other flavoring you love in place of the vanilla extract.

Directions:

i. Slice the cream cheese into 8 cubes; place in the bowl of a stand mixer or food processor. Add the butter and coconut oil and use the whisk attachment for the stand mixer to blend until smooth, or process in the food processor until smooth.

ii. Stir in the stevia, vanilla, and salt.

iii. Pour the cheesecake mixture into 4 regular-size or 8 mini paper muffin cups. Garnish with toasted coconut chips, if desired. Freeze for 5 minutes or place in the refrigerator for up to 1 hour to firm up.

DAY 6

Breakfast: BULLETPROOF COFFEE / TEA

Lunch: Stuffed Peppers

Yield: 4 servings

Nutritional info

Calories 587, fat 51.8, fiber 3, carbs 8.8, protein 23.3

Ingredients:

- ☐ 4 large green bell peppers
- ☐ 1/2 cup (4 ounces/115 g) butter
- ☐ 2 tablespoons thinly sliced green onions
- ☐ 1 clove garlic, minced
- ☐ 2 cups (8 ounces/225 g) riced cauliflower
- ☐ ½ cup (4 fluid ounces/120 ml) beef bone broth
- ☐ 8 ounces (225 g) ground beef
- ☐ 8 ounces (225 g) ground pork
- ☐ 1 medium tomato, chopped
- ☐ 1 tablespoon tamari
- ☐ ½ teaspoon fine sea salt
- ☐ ½ teaspoon garlic powder
- ☐ ½ teaspoon onion powder
- ☐ ½ teaspoon paprika
- ☐ ¼ teaspoon ground black pepper
- ☐ 3 ounces (85 g) mozzarella cheese, shredded

Directions:

i. Preheat the oven to 350°F (177°C). Grease a 9-inch (23-cm) square baking dish.

ii. Slice the top off of each bell pepper and trim the base to a flat edge so that the peppers will stand up. Carefully remove the core, seeds, and ribs, keeping the peppers intact. Arrange the peppers in the prepared baking dish.

iii. In a deep skillet over low heat, melt the butter. Add the green onions and garlic and cook for 2 to 3 minutes, until softened.

iv. Increase the heat to medium-low and add the riced cauliflower. Cook for 2 to 3 minutes, stirring often, until the cauliflower is lightly cooked and the butter is well mixed in.

v. Pour in the broth and increase the heat to medium. Simmer for 8 to 12 minutes, until the liquid is absorbed.

vi. Meanwhile, in a separate large skillet over medium heat, cook the ground beef and pork until lightly browned, using a spatula to break apart the meat, 7 to 8 minutes. Drain any excess water, if needed. Add the tomato, tamari, salt, and spices and stir to combine.

vii. Add the cauliflower mixture to the meat mixture; stir to combine. Spoon the meat and cauliflower mixture into the peppers and top with the mozzarella.

viii.	Bake for 25 to 30 minutes, until the tops are golden. If you want the tops extra brown, broil for an additional 1 to 2 minutes.

> **Note**
>
> You can either purchase pre-riced cauliflower (often called cauliflower rice) or make it yourself. To make it, pulse cauliflower florets in a food processor for 30 seconds to 1 minute. Watch it closely; you want the cauliflower grated and approximately rice-sized, but not too fine. You can also use the large holes on a box grater to grate the cauliflower into rice-like pieces.

Dinner: Pasta Carbonara

Yield: 4 servings

With zero-carb noodles, you can enjoy the rich and creamy flavor of this dish anytime. Because the eggs don't fully cook in the hot sauce, it's important to use pasteurized eggs in this recipe.

The Fat Burning Ketogenic Diet for Beginners

Nutritional info

Calories 469, fat 41.3, fiber 2, carbs 4.8, protein 19.8

Ingredients:

- [ ] 4 (7-ounce/200-g) packages fettuccine-style zero-carb shirataki noodles
- [ ] 6 egg yolks from pasteurized eggs
- [ ] 4 tablespoons (1 ounce/28 g) grated Parmesan cheese, divided
- [ ] ½ teaspoon coarse sea salt
- [ ] ¼ teaspoon ground black pepper
- [ ] ¼ cup plus 2 tablespoons (3 ounces/85 g) butter or MCT oil, divided
- [ ] 8 ounces (225 g) pancetta, diced
- [ ] 2 cloves garlic, peeled and smashed
- [ ] 1 to 2 tablespoons filtered water

Directions:

i. Rinse and drain the noodles. In a saucepan over high heat, boil the noodles in water for 1 to 2 minutes. Drain and set on paper towels to absorb the excess water.

ii. In a bowl, whisk together the egg yolks, 3 tablespoons of the Parmesan, salt, and pepper. Set aside.

iii. In a skillet over medium heat, heat 1 tablespoon of the butter. Add the pancetta and fry for 1 to 2 minutes. Add the garlic and sauté for about 1 minute, until fragrant. Add the remaining 5 tablespoons (2½ ounces/70 g) of butter and cook for 4 to 5 minutes, until the flavors are well absorbed. Remove the garlic cloves from the pan.

iv. Add the noodles to the skillet and toss to coat. Remove from the heat and add 1 tablespoon of water, then pour in the egg yolk mixture. Gently but rapidly toss together the noodles and sauce, allowing the residual heat from the pan to gently cook the sauce without scrambling the eggs. If desired, add another 1 tablespoon of water to thin the sauce and make it smoother.

v. Divide the pasta between 4 bowls and top with the remaining 1 tablespoon of Parmesan. Garnish with more pepper, if desired.

Note

To smash garlic, lay the peeled cloves on a flat surface, such as your kitchen counter. Lay the flat side of a chef's knife or other large knife across the garlic. Use the edge of your fist to smack the top of the knife, smashing the garlic.

Dessert: Vanilla Ice Cream

Yield: 2 1/2 cups (15 ounces/430 g) (1/2 cup/3 ounces/85 g per serving)

Never in my life did I think that eating ice cream could a) be good for me or b) generate weight loss. The ketogenic diet truly is amazing! Enjoying my favorite flavor, vanilla, with MCT oil for fat burning ketones, plus rich organic heavy cream, totally guilt-free is something I never imagined. Yet on the keto diet, it's real! I use an ice cream maker for this recipe, but you don't need one. I have had success simply freezing this ice cream in a freezer-safe glass storage container, then letting it defrost a bit before serving. This method won't give you the same texture as an ice cream maker, but it's a great option. I have also used this recipe to make ice pops, freezing the ice cream in ice pop molds that I run under warm water before removing.

Nutritional info

Calories 206, fat 20.4, fiber 2.6, carbs 2.2, protein 3.8

Ingredients:

- 6 egg yolks from pasteurized eggs
- 1 cup (8 fluid ounces/240 ml) heavy whipping cream
- 1 cup (8 fluid ounces/240 ml) almond milk

- ☐ ¼ cup (2 ounces/57 g) erythritol
- ☐ 1 tablespoon coconut oil
- ☐ 1 tablespoon MCT oil
- ☐ 2 teaspoons almond extract
- ☐ 1 teaspoon vanilla paste, or 2 teaspoons vanilla extract
- ☐ 1 teaspoon liquid stevia
- ☐ Pinch of sea salt

SPECIAL EQUIPMENT:

- ☐ Ice cream maker (optional)

Directions:

i. Place all the ingredients in a blender and blend on high for a few minutes.

ii. If using an ice cream maker, remove the freezer bowl for the ice cream maker from the freezer. Pour the ice cream base into the ice cream maker and churn, following the manufacturer's instructions.

iii. Eat right away or, if you prefer a more solid ice cream, freeze it for a bit longer in a freezer-safe glass container. I like to remove the ice cream from the freezer about 15 minutes before serving so that it softens a little.

iv. If using a glass container to make the ice cream, pour the ice cream base into the container and place in the freezer. Remove from the freezer every 30 minutes and stir vigorously with a whisk or beat with an electric mixer until it has the texture of soft-serve ice cream, 2 to 3 hours. If a firmer texture is desired, freeze longer.

Note

This recipe does not include the step of cooking the eggs, so it's important to use yolks from pasteurized, not raw, eggs. You can also temper the eggs and gently cook the mixture over very low heat, stirring constantly, and then chilling the mixture before freezing or churning it in an ice cream maker.

DAY 7

Breakfast: Egg, Bacon, Sun-Dried Tomato, and Feta Breakfast Muffins

Yield: 12 muffins (2 per serving)

These muffins are the best grab-and-go breakfast for busy weekday mornings. Make them on Sunday and you'll have breakfast for the whole week! They are perfect for picnics or hikes, and they can even be frozen. Add some chopped fresh spinach or kale to increase the carb content.

Nutritional info

Calories 432, fat 34.5, fiber 1.5, carbs 3.5, protein 25

Ingredients:

- ☐ Coconut oil, for the pan
- ☐ 20 slices thick-cut bacon, diced
- ☐ 10 eggs
- ☐ 1 cup (4 ounces/115 g) crumbled feta cheese
- ☐ 1 ounce (28 g) sun-dried tomatoes in oil, drained and sliced
- ☐ ¼ cup plus 2 tablespoons (3 ounces/85 g) coconut cream or heavy whipping cream
- ☐ ¼ teaspoon onion powder
- ☐ ¼ teaspoon garlic powder
- ☐ ¼ teaspoon fine sea salt
- ☐ ¼ teaspoon ground black pepper

Directions:

i. Preheat the oven to 350°F (177°C). Grease a 12-cup muffin pan with coconut oil.

ii. In a skillet over medium heat, fry the bacon for 5 to 7 minutes, until slightly crispy; do not overcook. Transfer to a bowl to cool, reserving the bacon fat in the pan.

iii. In a medium bowl, whisk the eggs. Add the rest of the ingredients, including the bacon, to the bowl and stir gently to combine.

iv. Divide the egg mixture among the greased muffin cups, using ¼ to ⅓ cup per muffin.

v. Bake until set, about 20 minutes.

Lunch: Shrimp Pad Thai

Yield: 2 servings

If I had to eat just one thing for the rest of my life, it would probably be Pad Thai. I've always loved this dish—especially when it comes from an open-air market in Bangkok, fresh and hot out of a wok and served in banana leaves and wrapped in newspaper. This recipe re-creates all those creamy, nutty, tangy, tart, sour, sweet, and spicy flavors without the palm sugar and tamarind in the original dish.

Nutritional info

Calories 780, fat 69.5, fiber 5.5, carbs 12.5, protein 27

Ingredients:

- 1 tablespoon coconut oil
- 2 eggs, whisked
- ½ cup (3½ ounces/100 g) mung beans, rinsed and drained
- 12 uncooked medium to large shrimp, thawed if frozen, peeled and deveined
- 2 (7-ounce/200-g) packages fettuccine-style zero-carb shirataki noodles
- 1 tablespoon crushed almonds
- 1 tablespoon chopped fresh cilantro
- 1 tablespoon sliced green onions

PAD THAI SAUCE:

- 2 tablespoons unsweetened almond butter
- 2 tablespoons coconut oil
- 2 tablespoons mayonnaise
- 2 tablespoons tahini
- 2 tablespoons tamari
- 1 tablespoon freshly squeezed lime juice
- 2 teaspoons fish sauce

- ☐ ½ teaspoon ginger juice, or 1 teaspoon grated fresh ginger
- ☐ ½ teaspoon liquid stevia (optional)
- ☐ ¼ teaspoon hot sauce, or a pinch of cayenne pepper
- ☐ 1 teaspoon granulated stevia or erythritol
- ☐ ½ teaspoon fine sea salt
- ☐ ¼ teaspoon garlic powder

Directions:

i. In a small skillet over medium heat, melt 1 tablespoon of coconut oil. Add the eggs and cook through to make a thin omelet. Remove from the pan and set aside to cool. When cool, slice into thin ribbons.

ii. In the same skillet over medium heat, fry the mung beans for 2 to 3 minutes. Add the shrimp and cook for 2 to 3 minutes, until bright pink and cooked through, being careful not to overcook.

iii. Rinse and drain the noodles. In a saucepan over high heat, boil the noodles in water for 1 to 2 minutes. Drain the noodles and set on paper towels to absorb the excess water.

iv. Put all the ingredients for the sauce in a food processor and process until well combined. Combine the noodles with the sauce.

v. Divide the sauced noodles between 2 plates. Top each plate with half of the egg ribbons, beans, shrimp, almonds, cilantro, and onions.

Dinner: Ceviche with Spicy Mayo

Yield: 2 main-dish servings or 4 appetizer servings

Ceviche is one of my favorite foods and enjoying it with MCT oil and mayo takes it to the next level of delicious. This recipe makes four appetizers or two main courses.

Nutritional info

Calories 417, fat 36.3, fiber 2.5, carbs 4.5, protein 18.3

Ingredients:

- 12 ounces (340 g) halibut or other white fish fillets, chopped into ½-inch (1.25-cm) cubes
- 3 green onions, green parts only, thinly sliced
- 1 cup (8 fluid ounces/240 ml) freshly squeezed lime juice, plus more if needed
- 1 medium-sized ripe avocado, peeled and cut into ½-inch (1.25-cm) cubes
- 2 to 3 green jalapeño peppers or serrano chilies, finely chopped

- ☐ ¼ cup (¼ ounce/7 g) finely chopped fresh cilantro
- ☐ ¼ cup (2 fluid ounces/60 ml) MCT oil or olive oil
- ☐ ¼ teaspoon fine sea salt
- ☐ ¼ cup (2 ounces/55 g) mayonnaise
- ☐ 1 teaspoon hot sauce

Directions:

i. Arrange the fish in a single layer in an 8-inch (20-cm) square baking dish or glass bowl. Sprinkle with the onions and pour the lime juice over the top, making sure the fish is fully covered in the juice; if it isn't, add more juice. Cover and place in the refrigerator for 4 to 5 hours to marinate.

ii. Remove the fish from the refrigerator and verify that it is thoroughly "cooked"; it should be opaque in the center. Return it to the refrigerator to marinate longer, if needed.

iii. Drain and transfer the fish to a bowl. Add the avocado, jalapeño, cilantro, oil, and salt; stir gently to combine.

iv. Make the spicy mayo: In another bowl, combine the mayonnaise and hot sauce.

v. Serve the fish immediately, accompanied by the spicy mayo.

Dessert: Avocado Tzatziki Dip

Yield: 4 servings

Mediterranean diets incorporate wonderful fats, including lots of olive oil. I created a version of tzatziki with avocado and avocado oil for a fun twist on this Greek favorite. It makes for a great alternative to guacamole!

Nutritional info

Calories 332, fat 31.3, fiber 4.3, carbs 10.8, protein 4.8

Ingredients:

- ½ large cucumber, peeled
- ½ teaspoon fine sea salt
- 1 medium-sized ripe avocado, halved and pitted
- ½ cup (4 ounces/115 g) Greek yogurt
- ½ cup (4 ounces/115 g) sour cream
- 2 tablespoons finely chopped fresh dill
- 1 tablespoon freshly squeezed lemon juice
- 1 clove garlic, minced
- ¼ teaspoon ground black pepper
- ¼ cup (2 fluid ounces/60 ml) avocado oil
- ¼ cup (1¼ ounces/35 g) slivered
- Kalamata olives (optional) Fresh mint leaves, for garnish (optional)

Directions:

i. Peel the cucumber and scrape out the seeds. Grate the seeded cucumber, then place it in a colander and set over a bowl to drain. Stir in the salt and allow to sit, stirring occasionally, until the moisture drains out, 10 to 15 minutes. Wrap in a clean dish towel or paper towels and squeeze out the excess water.

ii. Scoop the avocado flesh into another bowl and mash until very smooth. Stir in the salted cucumber, yogurt, sour cream, dill, lemon juice, garlic, and pepper. Taste and season with additional salt, if needed.

iii. Transfer the dip to a wide serving bowl. Drizzle with the avocado oil and sprinkle with the olives, if using. Garnish with mint leaves, if desired.

DAY 8

Breakfast: BULLETPROOF COFFEE / TEA

Lunch: Sun-Dried Tomato Fettuccine

Yield: 4 servings

This is one of the most delicious pastas—and very filling! Use fettuccine-style shirataki noodles or omit the pasta altogether and serve the sauce over cooked green cabbage ribbons or zucchini noodles.

Nutritional info

Calories 520, fat 48.8, fiber 3, carbs 9.3, protein 10.8

Ingredients:

- ☐ 4 (7-ounce/200-g) packages fettuccine-style zero-carb shirataki noodles
- ☐ ⅓ cup (2⅔ fluid ounces/80 ml) almond milk
- ☐ 1 (8-ounce/225-g) package cream cheese
- ☐ ½ cup (4 ounces/115 g) mayonnaise
- ☐ 1 cup (5¼ ounces/150 g) crumbled feta cheese
- ☐ 2 ounces (56 g) sun-dried tomatoes in oil, drained
- ☐ ½ teaspoon fine sea salt
- ☐ ¼ teaspoon garlic powder
- ☐ Cracked black pepper, for garnish (optional)
- ☐ Red pepper flakes, for garnish (optional)

Directions:

i. Rinse and drain the noodles. In a saucepan over high heat, boil the noodles in water for 1 to 2 minutes. Drain and set on paper towels to absorb the excess water.

ii. If desired, transfer the noodles to a cutting board and chop into 2-inch (5-cm) segments. Set aside.

iii. Place the milk, cream cheese, mayonnaise, feta, sun-dried tomatoes, salt, and garlic powder in a food processor and pulse until well combined and creamy.

iv. Pour the sauce into a medium saucepan and cook over low heat until warmed through. Add the noodles and mix well.

v. Divide the sauced noodles between 2 plates. Serve topped with cracked black pepper and red pepper flakes, if desired.

Dinner: Trio of Beef Sliders

Yield: 4 servings

Sliders are one of the most fun ways to enjoy burgers! I often make these for groups or parties, and everyone loves them. Depending on the type of gathering, I either set up a topping bar so that each person can select their own toppings, or assemble the trios of sliders so that everyone can try all three kinds.

Nutritional info

Calories 878, fat 78.8, fiber 5, carbs 8, protein 48

Ingredients:

- 1 ½ pounds (680 g) ground beef
- ½ medium onion, finely chopped
- 1 teaspoon cayenne pepper
- 1 teaspoon garlic powder
- 1 teaspoon paprika
- 1 or 2 drops liquid stevia, or 1 teaspoon erythritol
- 1 teaspoon fine sea salt
- ½ teaspoon ground black pepper
- 1 teaspoon maple flavoring, or 1 tablespoon sugar-free maple syrup

TOPPINGS:

- 4 slices bacon

The Fat Burning Ketogenic Diet for Beginners

- ☐ ¼ cup (2 ounces/55 g) unsalted butter
- ☐ 1 clove garlic, minced
- ☐ ½ cup (1 1/4 ounces/40 g) cremini or white mushrooms, diced
- ☐ 2 ounces (55 g) blue cheese, crumbled
- ☐ 1 avocado, peeled and pitted
- ☐ 1 teaspoon freshly squeezed lime juice
- ☐ ¼ teaspoon garlic powder
- ☐ Pinch of cayenne pepper
- ☐ ½ teaspoon fine sea salt
- ☐ ¼ cup (2 ounces/55 g) Special Burger Sauce or mayonnaise
- ☐ 4 slices cheddar or Gouda cheese
- ☐ 2 unsweetened medium to large dill pickles, sliced into rounds
- ☐ 12 butter lettuce leaves

Directions:

i. In a bowl, mix together the ground beef, onion, cayenne, garlic powder, paprika, stevia, 1 teaspoon salt, and ½ teaspoon pepper.

ii. Remove 8 ounces (225 g) of the meat mixture to a separate bowl and mix with the maple flavoring. Form four 2-ounce (55-g) sliders, each about 2 inches (5 cm) thick.

iii. From the remaining meat mixture, make eight 2-ounce (55-g) sliders.

iv. Heat a grill pan or heavy skillet (cast iron works well here) to medium-high heat. Grill the sliders for 4 to 5 minutes on each side for medium-done burgers, or to your desired level of doneness. Alternatively, you can grill the sliders on a gas or charcoal grill preheated to high heat for 5 to 6 minutes per side for medium-done burgers, or to your desired level of doneness. Set aside to rest.

v. Prepare the toppings: In a medium skillet over medium heat, fry the bacon for 3 to 4 minutes, until moderately crispy. Set aside.

vi. In a saucepan over medium heat, melt the butter. Add the garlic and sauté for 1 to 2 minutes, until fragrant. Add the mushrooms and sauté for 3 to 4 minutes. Sprinkle with the blue cheese and allow it to melt while blending it into the mushrooms. Set aside.

vii. Prepare guacamole by mashing together the avocado flesh, lime juice, garlic powder, cayenne, and ½ teaspoon salt.

viii. Assemble the 3 types of sliders: Top each of the 4 maple sliders with 1 tablespoon of Special Burger Sauce, a slice of cheddar, a slice of bacon, and pickles. Top 4 more sliders with the guacamole. Top the last 4 sliders with the mushroom and blue cheese mixture.

ix. Place each slider on a lettuce leaf and arrange one of each type of slider on each plate.

Dessert: Tzatziki Dip

Yield: 4 servings

Full-fat Greek yogurt is a creamy treat that can be enjoyed in moderation on a ketogenic diet, as it provides tons of fat and probiotics. This is a fantastic dip or dinner side; it's great in my Pork Gyro Lettuce Wraps with Quick Pickled Red Onions as a dip with endive leaves or crudités, or simply served alongside grilled meat or a tossed salad.

Nutritional info

Calories 217, fat 19, fiber 0.8, carbs 7.3, protein 5.3

Ingredients:

- ½ large cucumber, peeled
- ½ teaspoon fine sea salt
- 1 cup (8 ounces/225 g) plain Greek yogurt
- 1 cup (8 ounces/225 g) sour cream
- 2 tablespoons finely chopped fresh dill, plus more for garnish
- 1 tablespoon finely chopped fresh mint, plus more for garnish
- 1 tablespoon freshly squeezed lemon juice
- 1 clove garlic, minced

- ☐ ¼ teaspoon ground black pepper
- ☐ ¼ cup (2 fluid ounces/60 ml) olive oil
- ☐ ¼ cup (1¼ ounces/35 g) slivered Kalamata olives (optional)

Directions:

i. Peel the cucumber and scrape out the seeds. Grate the seeded cucumber, then place it in a colander and set over a bowl to drain. Stir in the salt and allow to sit, stirring occasionally, until the moisture drains out, 10 to 15 minutes. Wrap in a clean dish towel or paper towels and squeeze out the excess water.

ii. In another bowl, stir together the salted cucumber, yogurt, sour cream, dill, mint, lemon juice, garlic, and pepper. Taste and season with additional salt, if needed.

iii. Transfer the dip to a wide serving bowl. Drizzle with the olive oil and sprinkle with the olives, if using. Garnish with additional dill and mint.

DAY 9

Breakfast: Savory Brie

Yield: 2 servings (3 crêpes per serving)

I love cheese and mushrooms together—especially in a savory crêpe! This recipe reminds me of a cheese and mushroom quesadilla as well. I use regular white or brown mushrooms, but you can use varieties like chanterelles or morels if you prefer. Eat these crêpes for breakfast or dinner!

Nutritional info

Calories 729, fat 65.5, fiber 3, carbs 11, protein 28

Ingredients:

CRÊPES:

- ☐ 5 eggs
- ☐ ⅔ cup (5½ fluid ounces/160 ml) almond milk
- ☐ 2 tablespoons coconut flour
- ☐ 1 or 2 drops liquid stevia (optional)
- ☐ 3 tablespoons coconut oil or unsalted butter, for the pan

FILLING:

- ☐ 1 tablespoon coconut oil

- [ ] 1 clove garlic, crushed
- [ ] 1 cup (2.6 ounces/75 g) sliced mushrooms
- [ ] 1 cup (1¼ ounces/35 g) fresh spinach, chopped
- [ ] ¼ teaspoon fine sea salt
- [ ] ¼ teaspoon ground black pepper
- [ ] 4 ounces (115 g) triple cream Brie, sliced into 12 sections
- [ ] 2 tablespoons Sugar-Free Glaze for drizzling

Directions:

i. Prepare the crêpes: In a mixing bowl or the bowl of a stand mixer, combine the eggs, milk, coconut flour, and stevia, if using. Beat together with a handheld electric mixer or stand mixer.

ii. In a small skillet over high heat, melt 3 tablespoons of coconut oil. When hot, pour 2 tablespoons to ¼ cup of the batter into the pan, rotating the pan to spread the batter into a thin layer. When cooked on one side (about 1 minute), flip and cook on the other side. Remove from the pan and keep warm. Repeat with the remaining batter, making a total of 6 crêpes.

iii. Make the filling: In a medium skillet over medium heat, melt 1 tablespoon of coconut oil. Add the garlic and cook for 1 to 2 minutes, until fragrant. Add the mushrooms and cook for 4 to 5 minutes, until nicely browned; be careful not to overcrowd the mushrooms as you cook them. Once browned, add the spinach and cook for 2 to 3 minutes, until cooked. Season with the salt and pepper.

iv. Return the pan in which you cooked the crêpes to the stovetop over medium-low heat. Lay a crêpe flat in the pan. Add about one-sixth of the mushroom and spinach filling and layer with 2 slices of Brie. Fold the crêpe in half or into a triangle by folding in both sides. Flip over and cook until the cheese is melted. Repeat with the remaining crêpes and filling.

v. Plate the crêpes and drizzle 1 tablespoon of the glaze over each serving.

Lunch: Zucchini Lasagna

Yield: 6 servings

A keto spin on a classic family lunch! In this dish, sliced zucchini replaces sheets of pasta. It works best when as much water as possible is removed from the zucchini.

Nutritional info

Calories 586, fat 50.5, fiber 0.7, carbs 6, protein 29

Ingredients:

NOODLES:

- [ ] 2 medium to large zucchini, each sliced lengthwise into 6 long slices (a mandoline slicer works well)
- [ ] 1 to 2 tablespoons fine sea salt
- [ ] 1/2 cup (4 ounces/115 g) unsalted butter, divided
- [ ] 1 pound (455 g) ground beef
- [ ] ¼ cup (2 ounces/55 g) sliced green onions
- [ ] 1 clove garlic, minced
- [ ] ½ teaspoon red pepper flakes
- [ ] 12 cherry tomatoes, quartered
- [ ] 2 tablespoons finely chopped fresh basil, plus extra leaves for garnish
- [ ] 2 tablespoons finely chopped fresh oregano
- [ ] ½ teaspoon fine sea salt
- [ ] ¼ teaspoon ground black pepper
- [ ] 12 ounces (340 g) cream cheese, softened
- [ ] ½ cup plus 2 tablespoons
- [ ] (21/2 ounces/70 g) grated Parmesan cheese, divided
- [ ] ½ cup (2 ounces/55 g) shredded mozzarella cheese
- [ ] 2 egg yolks

Directions:

i. Preheat the oven to 375°F (190°C).

ii. Salt the zucchini with 1 to 2 tablespoons of salt. Set the slices in a colander to drain for 10 to 15 minutes, then rinse the zucchini and wipe off the salt with paper towels. Meanwhile, prepare the rest of the ingredients for the lasagna.

iii. In a large skillet over medium-low heat, melt ¼ cup (2 ounces/55 g) of the butter. Add the ground beef and cook until browned, breaking apart the meat as it cooks, 6 to 7 minutes.

iv. In a medium saucepan over medium heat, melt the remaining ¼ cup (2 ounces/55 g) of butter. Add the green onions, garlic, and red pepper flakes and sauté for 1 to 2 minutes. Add the tomatoes and stir to combine.

v. Add the browned ground beef to the green onion mixture and stir together.

vi. Stir in the basil, oregano, ½ teaspoon salt, and pepper, then slide the pan off the heat.

vii. In a bowl, mix together the cream cheese, ½ cup (2 ounces/55g) of the Parmesan, mozzarella, and egg yolks.

viii. Have on hand a 10-inch (12.5-cm) to 12-inch (17.5-cm) ovenproof skillet. To layer the lasagna in the pan, spread half of the beef and tomato mixture over the bottom of the pan. Layer on 6 zucchini slices, trimming as necessary, then spread half the cheese mixture

ix. Cover with aluminum foil and bake for 1 hour, removing the foil after 45 minutes. If desired, turn the oven to broil after 1 hour and broil for 1 to 2 minutes, until the top is brown and crispy. Garnish with fresh basil leaves.

Dinner: Easy Keto Meatloaf

Yield: 6 servings

Meatloaf is traditionally made with quite a bit of ketchup and Worcestershire sauce. If you can find a healthy sugar-free ketchup, you can use it in this recipe along with Homemade Worcestershire Sauce

Nutritional info

Calories 675, fat 55, fiber 1.2, carbs 4.3, protein 40

Ingredients:

- 5 eggs
- 3 ounces (90 g) bacon
- 17 ounces (500 g) ground beef
- 17 ounces (500 g) ground pork
- 1/4 cup plus 2 tablespoons (3 ounces/85 g) butter

The Fat Burning Ketogenic Diet for Beginners

- ½ cup (2 1/2 ounces/70 g) chopped onions
- 1 clove garlic, minced
- 2 medium tomatoes, chopped
- 2 tablespoons Homemade Worcestershire Sauce
- 1/4 cup plus 2 tablespoons (1½ ounces/40 g) almond flour
- 2 tablespoons chopped fresh parsley, plus more for garnish

Directions:

i. Preheat the oven to 350°F (177°C). Grease a 9 by 5-inch (23 by 13-cm) loaf pan.

ii. Place 3 eggs in a saucepan of water and bring to a boil. Boil for 6 to 7 minutes, then remove the pan from the heat. Let the eggs sit in the hot water for an additional 10 minutes. Rinse under cold water until chilled, then peel. Set aside.

iii. Meanwhile, in a skillet over medium heat, fry the bacon for 3 to 4 minutes, until cooked but not crispy. Remove from the pan, chop, and place in a bowl.

iv. In the same skillet in which you cooked the bacon, brown the ground beef and pork until cooked through, breaking apart the meat with a wooden spoon, 6 to 8 minutes. Drain the excess fat, if needed.

v. In a large saucepan over low heat, melt the butter. Add the onions and garlic and cook for 2 to 3 minutes, until lightly cooked. Add the tomatoes and ground meat to the pan and mix well. Add the Worcestershire sauce and cook for about 2 more minutes, then transfer the mixture to a large mixing bowl and let cool slightly.

vi. To the bowl with the ground meat mixture, add the bacon, flour, parsley, and 2 remaining eggs. Using your hands, mix the ingredients together, then place half of the mixture in the prepared loaf pan. Place the 3 hard-boiled eggs in a row on the meat mixture and top with the remaining meat mixture. Cook for 1 hour or until the meat is cooked through and reaches an internal temperature of 160°F (70°C). Garnish with chopped parsley before serving.

Dessert: Keto Ghanoush

Yield: 2 servings

Mediterranean food emphasizes low-carb and high-fat—concepts that are keto-friendly and provide a ton of recipe inspiration for me! This baba ghanoush is great with cucumber slices or pork rinds. The standard eggplant for baba ghanoush is a globe eggplant, which is generally 7 to 8 inches long (18 to 20 cm) and weighs about 1 pound (2.5 kg).

The Fat Burning Ketogenic Diet for Beginners

Nutritional info

Calories 430, fat 42.5, fiber 6, carbs 11.5, protein 4.5

Ingredients:

- ½ globe eggplant (8 ounces/225 g), top removed, sliced into
- 6 long sections
- 1 teaspoon fine sea salt, divided
- 1 cup (4¼ ounces/120 g) quartered and sliced zucchini
- 2 cloves garlic
- 5 tablespoons (2½ fluid ounces/75 ml) olive oil, divided
- 2 tablespoons tahini
- 1 tablespoon freshly squeezed lemon juice
- ¼ teaspoon ground cumin
- ¼ teaspoon ground black pepper
- ¼ teaspoon paprika, for garnish
- 1 tablespoon chopped fresh parsley, for garnish

Directions:

i. Preheat the broiler to medium.
ii. Place the eggplant in a colander or on a bed of paper towels. Sprinkle on both sides with ½ teaspoon of the salt and let sit for

10 to 15 minutes. Wipe well with paper towels to dry the eggplant and remove the salt.

iii. Arrange the salted eggplant, zucchini, and garlic on a rimmed baking sheet. Drizzle with 1 tablespoon of the olive oil.

iv. Broil the vegetables for 10 to 12 minutes, until softened. Using a spoon, scrape the flesh of the eggplant out of the skin and into a food processor.

v. To the food processor, add the roasted zucchini and garlic cloves, along with the remaining ½ teaspoon of salt, 3 tablespoons of the olive oil, tahini, lemon juice, cumin, and pepper. Blend until smooth. Taste and adjust for seasoning.

vi. Transfer the baba ghanoush to a serving bowl. Drizzle with the remaining 1 tablespoon of olive oil, sprinkle with the paprika, and garnish with parsley. The baba ghanoush will keep in the refrigerator for up to 3 days.

DAY 10

Breakfast: BULLETPROOF COFFEE /TEA

Lunch: Hot Wings with Blue Cheese and Celery

Yield: 3 servings

Chicken wings are a restaurant favorite and an excellent keto meal to make at home. Even without the usual batter and breading, these wings taste fantastic! Surprisingly, this is a super-keto and low-carb recipe, with only 1 percent carbohydrate.

Nutritional info

Calories 686, fat 60, fiber 1.3, carbs 8.3, protein 28.3

Ingredients:

- ½ cup (4 ounces/115 g) butter
- ½ cup (4 fluid ounces/120 ml) medium-hot hot sauce
- 1 tablespoon apple cider vinegar
- Sea salt and ground black pepper
- Refined coconut oil or lard, for frying
- 1 pound (455 g) chicken wings, cut into wingettes and drumettes
- 6 medium stalks celery, chopped into 4 segments each

- ☐ 2 tablespoons Blue Cheese Dressing

Directions:

i. In a medium saucepan over low heat, melt the butter. Add the hot sauce, vinegar, and salt and pepper to taste.

ii. If using a deep-fryer, heat the coconut oil in the deep-fryer to 338°F (170°C). Alternatively, heat 2 inches (5 cm) of coconut oil in a deep heavy skillet over medium-high heat to 375°F (190°C). Pat the wings dry and season with a bit of salt and pepper.

iii. If using a deep-fryer, fry for 8 to 10 minutes, then remove to a plate lined with paper towels and let cool. Increase the oil temperature to 375°F (190°C) and fry the wings again for 30 seconds to 1 minute. If cooking the wings on the stovetop, fry until crispy and cooked through, about 10 minutes.

iv. Remove the wings from the oil and coat with the hot sauce mixture.

v. Divide the wings between 3 plates and serve each with 8 celery

---

Tip

When I make these succulent wings in a deep-fryer, I like to fry them twice. The first fry is at the near-highest setting. Then I remove the wings and let them cool. Then, I fry them again for a few minutes at the highest setting. The result is crispy, not soggy, wings.

---

segments and 1 tablespoon of the blue cheese dressing.

Dinner: Keto Moussaka

Yield: 6 servings

When my husband and I were in Greece for our honeymoon, I ate the most delicious moussaka, and I knew that I had to make a version for this cookbook! Eggplant is such a delectable vegetable, and this combination of eggplant, spices, and white sauce is going to make for a family favorite.

Nutritional info

Calories 757, fat 60.6, fiber 3, carbs 13, protein 37.5

Ingredients:

MEAT SAUCE:

- ☐ 2 tablespoons olive oil

- ☐ 2 pounds (910 g) ground beef
- ☐ 2 teaspoons dried oregano leaves
- ☐ 1 teaspoon ground Ceylon cinnamon or regular cinnamon
- ☐ ½ teaspoon ground nutmeg
- ☐ 1 teaspoon fine sea salt
- ☐ ½ teaspoon ground black pepper
- ☐ 1 onion, diced
- ☐ 3 cloves garlic, minced
- ☐ 1 cup (5 1/2 ounces/160 g) quartered grape tomatoes
- ☐ 1 cup (8 fluid ounces/240 ml) beef bone broth

EGGPLANT LAYER:

- ☐ 1 large eggplant (about 1 pound/ 455 g)

KETO WHITE SAUCE:

- ☐ 2 tablespoons butter
- ☐ 2 cups (16 fluid ounces/480 ml) heavy whipping cream
- ☐ 6 egg yolks
- ☐ ¼ teaspoon ground nutmeg
- ☐ ¼ teaspoon fine sea salt
- ☐ ¼ teaspoon ground black pepper
- ☐ ½ cup (2 ounces/55 g) grated Parmesan cheese, divided

Directions:

i. Preheat the oven to 375°F (190°C).

ii. Make the meat sauce: Heat the olive oil in a large skillet over medium heat. Add the ground beef, oregano, cinnamon, nutmeg, salt, and pepper; cook the meat, breaking it apart, until browned but not cooked through, about 5 minutes. Drain the excess moisture from the meat, leaving 1 tablespoon in the skillet, and remove the meat to a bowl.

iii. Return the skillet to the stovetop. Add the onion and garlic and cook over medium heat until translucent, about 5 minutes. Stir in the cooked beef, tomatoes, and broth and simmer until thickened, about 10 minutes.

iv. Cut the eggplant lengthwise into 1/8-inch (32-mm) slices.

v. Make the white sauce: In a heavy-bottomed pot over low heat, melt the butter. Whisk in the cream, egg yolks, nutmeg, salt, pepper, and half of the Parmesan cheese. Cook, while whisking, until thickened, about 10 minutes.

vi. To assemble the moussaka: Ladle enough of the meat sauce into a 9-inch (23-cm) square baking dish to lightly cover the bottom. Top with half of the eggplant slices in an even layer, trimming as necessary to make the eggplant fit. Top with half of the remaining meat sauce, followed by the remaining eggplant slices, and then the remaining meat sauce. Pour the white sauce over the top, spreading it into an even layer. Sprinkle with the remaining Parmesan cheese.

vii. Bake until bubbling and golden, 45 to 50 minutes. Tent with aluminum foil if the top starts to get too brown. Allow to sit for 10 minutes before slicing and serving.

Dessert: Ketogenic Hummus

Yield: 3 servings

The recipe makes three servings, but it is very low in calories and moderate in carbs, so it could be divided into two servings instead of three. Pork rinds or cucumber crackers make a delicious pairing. If you prefer a sweeter, less-intense garlic flavor, roast a couple of garlic cloves whole in their skins in a covered baking dish in a 400°F (205°C) oven for 45 minutes before making the hummus.

Nutritional info

Calories 211, fat 19, fiber 3, carbs 8.3, protein 3.3

Ingredients:

The Fat Burning Ketogenic Diet for Beginners

- [ ] 2½ cups (10 ounces/285 g) chopped cauliflower florets (about ½ medium head)
- [ ] 1 cup (5 ounces/140 g) sliced zucchini (about 1 medium)
- [ ] ¼ cup (1¼ ounces/35 g) tahini
- [ ] 3 tablespoons freshly squeezed lemon juice
- [ ] 3 tablespoons olive oil, divided
- [ ] 1 clove garlic (or more to taste)
- [ ] ½ teaspoon fine sea salt
- [ ] ¼ teaspoon ground black pepper
- [ ] ¼ teaspoon paprika, for garnish
- [ ] Chopped fresh parsley, for garnish (optional)
- [ ] Cucumber slices, for serving (optional)

Directions:

i. Boil the cauliflower in a medium to large saucepan full of water until soft, about 10 minutes. Add the zucchini and cook for another 5 minutes. Remove and drain.

ii. Transfer the cauliflower and zucchini to a food processor. Add the tahini, lemon juice, 1 tablespoon of the olive oil, garlic, salt, and pepper and blend until smooth. Taste and adjust for seasoning.

iii. Place the hummus on a serving plate. Garnish with the paprika and parsley, if using, and drizzle with the remaining 2 tablespoons of olive oil. Serve with cucumber slices for dipping, if desired. The hummus will keep in the refrigerator for up to a week.

Get started with your 10-day Ketogenic plan today!

	BREAKFAST	**LUNCH**	**DINNER**	**DESSERT**
DAY 1	Avocado Bacon Devilled Eggs	Coconut Soup	Steak with Béarnaise Sauce	Lemon Curd
DAY 2	Bulletproof Coffee / Tea	Three-Cheese Macaroni	Feta-Stuffed Meatballs	Cinnamon Custard
DAY 3	Baked Eggs Benedict Casserole	Bacon Pesto Pasta	Thai Chicken Satay	Chocolate Mint Mousse
DAY 4	Bulletproof Coffee / Tea	Pasta Bolognese	Steak with Green Peppercorn Sauce	Instant Chia Pudding
DAY 5	Breakfast Crêpes	Fettuccine Alfredo with Grilled Shrimp	Duck Rillettes	Cheesecake Fat Bombs
DAY 6	Bulletproof Coffee / Tea	Stuffed Peppers	Pasta Carbonara	Vanilla Ice Cream
DAY 7	Egg, Bacon, Sun-Dried Tomato, and Feta Breakfast Muffins	Shrimp Pad Thai	Ceviche with Spicy Mayo	Avocado Tzatziki Dip
DAY 8	Bulletproof Coffee / Tea	Sun-Dried Tomato Fettuccine	Trio of Beef Sliders	Tzatziki Dip

The Fat Burning Ketogenic Diet for Beginners

DAY 9	Savory Brie	Zucchini Lasagna	Easy Keto Meatloaf	Keto Ghanoush
DAY 10	Bulletproof Coffee / Tea	Hot Wings with Blue Cheese and Celery	Keto Moussaka	Ketogenic Hummus

CONCLUSION

If you've made it this far, then you must be really excited to get started on the path to a healthier and fitter body, thanks to the keto diet. It will be a challenging journey as your body makes the natural changes to accommodate and transform for the better.

Do not expect results overnight. Remember that Rome was never built in a day, and your body will take some time to transform before you shed those pounds and are finally able to enjoy that great body. So be patient, stay motivated and never give up on your weight loss goals. All the best!

REFERENCES

Locke Hugehs, Women's Health (2018): *"These 5 Celebrities Are Obsessed with the Ketogenic Diet"*. Retrieved from https://www.womenshealthmag.com/weight-loss/g16641173/keto-diet-celebrities/

Kate Morgan, The Cut, (2018): *"What Exactly Is the Keto Diet, and Is It Safe?"* Retrieved from https://www.thecut.com/2018/01/what-is-keto-diet-foods-carbs-safety.html

Moira Lawler, Everyday Health (2018): *"12 Celebrities Who Can't Get Enough of the Ketogenic Diet"*. Retrieved from https://www.everydayhealth.com/ketogenic-diet/diet/celebrities-cant-get-enough-ketogenic-diet/

Perfect Keto, (2018): *"The Ultimate Start up Guide to The Ketogenic Diet"*. Retrieved from https://www.perfectketo.com/guide/ultimate-start-guide-ketogenic-diet/

Tarah Chieffi, Pop Sugar, (2018): *"Searching For Your Soul Mate Diet? Find Out If Keto or IF Is Right For You"*. Retrieved from https://www.popsugar.com/fitness/Intermittent-Fasting-vs-Keto-Diet-44436910

Ruled.me, (2013): *"A Comprehensive Beginner's Guide to the Ketogenic Diet"*. Retrieved from https://www.ruled.me/guide-keto-diet/

Paoli A., et.al. Department of Biomedical Sciences, University of Padova, Italy, (2012): *"Nutrition and Acne: Therapeutic Potential of Ketogenic Diets"*. Retrieved from https://www.ncbi.nlm.nih.gov/pubmed/22327146

John C. Newman, Anthony J. Covarrubias, Minghao Zhao et al., (2017): "Ketogenic Diet Reduces Midlife Mortality and Improves Memory in Aging Mice". Retrieved from https://www.cell.com/cell-metabolism/fulltext/S1550-4131(17)30489-8

Megan N. Roberts, Marita A. Wallace, Alexey A. Tomilov et al., (2017): "A Ketogenic Diet Extends Longevity and Healthspan in Adult Mice". Retrieved from https://www.cell.com/cell-metabolism/fulltext/S1550-4131(17)30490-4?code=cell-site

Bueno NB, de Melo IS, de Oliveira SL, da Rocha Ataide T., (2013): "Very-low-carbohydrate ketogenic diet v. low-fat diet for long-term weight loss: a meta-analysis of randomised controlled trials." Retrieved from https://www.ncbi.nlm.nih.gov/pubmed/23651522

Made in the USA
Middletown, DE
01 April 2019